S0-BOF-850

# THANDABANTU
## THE MAN WHO LOVED THE PEOPLE

### J. CAMERON FRASER
### FOREWORD BY LORD MACKAY

# THANDABANTU
## THE MAN WHO LOVED THE PEOPLE

J. CAMERON FRASER
FOREWORD BY LORD MACKAY

Belleville, Ontario, Canada

THANDABANTU: THE MAN WHO LOVED THE PEOPLE
Copyright © 2010, J. Cameron Fraser

*All Rights Reserved. No part of this publication may be reproduced, stored in a retrieval system or transmitted in any form or by any means—electronic, mechanical, photocopy, recording or any other—except for brief quotations in printed reviews, without the prior permission of the author.*

**Library and Archives Canada Cataloguing in Publication**

Fraser, J. Cameron (James Cameron), 1954-
      Thandabantu : the man who loved the people / J. Cameron Fraser.

Includes bibliographical references.
ISBN 978-1-55452-480-8 (pbk.).--ISBN 978-1-55452-481-5 (LSI ed.)

1. Fraser, James Samuel, 1913-1959. 2. Presbyterians--Scotland--Biography. 3. Missionaries--Scotland--Biography. 4. Presbyterians--Missions--Zimbabwe. I. Title.

BX9225.F73F72 2010     285'.2092     C2010-901777-3

**To order additional copies, visit:**
www.essencebookstore.com

**For more information, please contact:**
J. Cameron Fraser
www.SoS-Books.com
Available in the UK from
www.peterreynoldsbooks.com

*Guardian Books* is an imprint of *Essence Publishing,* a Christian Book Publisher dedicated to furthering the work of Christ through the written word. For more information, contact:
20 Hanna Court, Belleville, Ontario, Canada K8P 5J2
Phone: 1-800-238-6376 • Fax: (613) 962-3055
E-mail: info@essence-publishing.com
Web site: www.essence-publishing.com

For Matthias and James

# CONTENTS

# FOREWORD

I FIRST KNEW JAMES FRASER WHEN I WAS A SCHOOLBOY AND
he was a university student. My parents and I were
being entertained in the hospitable and beautiful home
of James' parents at Timaru in the lovely Highland village of Strathpeffer, where James' father ran a very suc-
cessful retail business.

James took me out to the lawn, sloping down to the
road and giving a very impressive setting to the house,
which I recollect as being of a colonial style. There we
occupied ourselves with wrestling and a variety of other
playful pursuits, which gave me a feeling of deep admi-
ration for James' talent with young people. In due
course this manifested itself more publicly when he
qualified as a teacher.

He had an even higher calling and became a student
for the ministry of the gospel. I heard him preach then
and after he was ordained. He was a clear, logical and

warm-hearted preacher with very well-prepared sermons that were structured to proceed from an introductory explanation of the background of the text to an analysis of its teaching and on to the lessons we should learn from it and which we should practice in our own lives.

Although he could have made a valuable contribution to the life of the church in Scotland, it was in Southern Rhodesia, now Zimbabwe, that James Fraser's lifework lay. He joined the staff of the Free Presbyterian mission with its headquarters in Ingwenya, founded there by the Reverend J.B. Radasi and carried on after his sad and sudden death by the Reverend John Tallach from Scotland.

James was a devoted missionary. He did his very best to bring all he could to know his Master, but he also equipped himself to assist the people by tending to their physical needs. His background in education enabled him also to make a massive contribution to the teaching of the people and to advancing those among them with a talent for higher education. His value in this sphere was clearly recognized by the civic authorities. The area of the mission extended out to Zenka and Mbuma, in the remote Shangani Reserve, with the challenges this posed to the strength and health of the missionaries.

The present account of James' lifework is told by Cameron, his affectionate son, who has followed his father into the gospel ministry, although in a very different field of labour. I commend it as full of interest to all who have a feeling for Africa.

As you will read, James Fraser, a servant of the Lord Jesus Christ, was taken from this work at an early age.

This left me and many others very sad and wondering at the divine purpose. What we know not now we shall know hereafter.

*Lord MacKay of Clashfern*

# PREFACE

THE 28TH OF MARCH 2009 WAS THE FIFTIETH ANNIVERSARY of my father's death. In 1967, his biography was published under the title *James Fraser: A Record of Missionary Endeavour in Rhodesia in the Twentieth Century.*[1] At least that is how the cover read. On an inside page, between the title and subtitle, were the words *The Man Who Loved the People,* based on his African nickname, *Thandabantu.* Thus, the title of the present work.

In early 2007, I was diagnosed with cancer. As this is written, more than two years and several treatments later, I am thankful to be in remission and back to full-time work, in answer to the prayers of many. It was during my illness that I determined to write a personal appreciation of my father as something of a legacy for my sons, Matthias and James. It was published as a series of articles in the *Banner of Truth* magazine

(March-May 2009) and now, with some minor revisions, in its present form.

Some who have already read this material say it has helped them better appreciate my passion for ministry to African refugees residing in our Canadian city. If this proves to be a secondary result of what I have written, it will be a welcome one.

I am grateful to my sisters, Elizabeth Fraser and Isobel Tallach, for their contributions and critique, and also to my uncle and aunt, Jan and Margaret van Woerden. Others who made helpful suggestions include the Reverend Dr. James Tallach (my cousin) and his cousins, Catherine and Margaret, as well as Miss C.M. Macaulay, a former colleague of my father's. The Reverend Bob de Moor, editor of the *Banner* (of the Christian Reformed Church), the Reverend Greg Sinclair, a fellow pastor (and former missionary in Mali), and Joel Belz, founder of *WORLD* magazine, offered objective evaluations of my original draft.

The gracious foreword is written by James MacKay, a family friend, whose own distinguished career includes having served as Lord Advocate of Scotland and then Lord Chancellor of the United Kingdom. Sonya Taekema provided invaluable help in preparing the manuscript, photographs and cover design for publication. Suzie Dalton drew the map of Zimbabwe. Dolina MacCuish kindly granted permission to use three photographs from her book *A Heart for Africa: The Story of Jean Nicolson—Missionary in Zimbabwe* (Glasgow: Free Presbyterian Publications, 2008). Grateful thanks are extended to all of the above.

My wife, Margaret, has been an unfailing source of

support and encouragement, especially during my recent illness. God has been merciful and gracious beyond imagining. I am thankful to him for so much, not least the memory of both my parents, which I seek to honour.

*An outline of present-day Zimbabwe with mission stations associated with my father (Ingwenya, Hope Fountain, Zenka, Mbuma) included*

THE COUNTRY IN WHICH MY FATHER MINISTERED WAS THEN known as Southern Rhodesia. Neighbouring Northern Rhodesia became Zambia in 1964. The following year, Rhodesian prime minister Ian Smith announced a unilateral declaration of independence from the United Kingdom, proclaiming that black majority rule would not come for "a thousand years." The white-majority government declared itself a republic in 1970.

A war of liberation ensued, resulting in the country officially gaining independence in 1980, with the new name of Zimbabwe and a government led by Robert Mugabe. Initial developments were promising, but by the time the Zimbabwean currency was taken off the market in April 2009, the one-time "breadbasket" of Africa had the highest inflation rate as well as the lowest life expectancy in the world, with a growing cholera epidemic and widespread starvation.[2] An attempted unity government formed with Mugabe's chief rival, Morgan Tsvangirai, following a disputed 2008 election, brought the situation there once again to world attention. It would be good if this review of my father's life in Southern Rhodesia more than half a century ago had as one of its effects the encouragement of prayerful concern for present-day Zimbabwe.

## MISSION BACKGROUND

The mission work into which my father was to enter began in a uniquely promising way. John Boyana Radasi grew up in the Transkei, a small region of what was then the British Cape Colony in South Africa. As a young man, he joined a choir, which took part in Queen Victoria's Diamond Jubilee celebrations in 1897. The choir travelled to the United States, where it is believed that John Radasi was converted, although he also had the benefit of a Christian upbringing. From there the story is told as follows by Jean Nicolson, who was herself later to play an important role in the mission's history:

> While he was in the United States, John Radasi made friends with another young African, James Saki. They heard that Scotland was a very religious country where there were good preachers, so they decided to go to Scotland on their way home...
> [They] duly arrived in Edinburgh, and after finding somewhere to stay, [made] their way to Lothian Road. There they stopped on the edge of the pavement, feeling rather lonely and sad. In the Lord's providence they stood opposite the

house of a Free Presbyterian lady, Mrs. Sinclair. Her son looked out the window and saw the two African men and was immediately interested; he had lived in South Africa for some years and had learned one of the African languages. He went outside to speak to them. After greeting them and asking them where they had come from, he invited the two men into his mother's house. Mrs. Sinclair welcomed them and quickly prepared tea. Mr. Radasi asked God's blessing on the food, and soon they were

*The Reverend John B. Radasi*

engaged in an interesting conversation which indicated that Mr. Radasi was a spiritually minded man. Mrs. Sinclair knew that the Rev. Neil Cameron, then a Free Presbyterian minister in Glasgow, was prayerfully interested in beginning foreign mission work. She sent him a telegram which read, 'I have your missionary'. Mr. Cameron replied, 'Send him along'.[3]

Thus were laid the foundations of the Free Presbyterian mission in Zimbabwe. After several years of training in the principles of the church, John Radasi was ordained to the ministry and returned to Africa, arriving in late December of 1904. Meanwhile, James Saki had left to join the Plymouth Brethren.

Mr. Radasi settled in Matabeleland, a region of Southern Rhodesia founded by the noted warrior Mzilikazi, who during the previous century had defied the fearsome Zulu chief Shaka and then fled north with a small group of followers. Mzilikazi met the Scottish pioneer missionary Robert Moffat, father-in-law of missionary-explorer David Livingstone. A friendship developed between the two men. In 1859, Moffat and his son received permission from Mzilikazi to begin a mission in what became known as Matabeleland.[4] Moffat worked under the auspices of the London Missionary Society, and one of the first mission stations established in Matabeleland was at Hope Fountain, which was later to play an important role in my father's life.

Southern Rhodesia was formed in 1898, named in honour of Cecil Rhodes of the British South Africa Company, comprising Matabeleland to the south and Mashonaland to the north. Rhodes invited the Fingos from Cape Colony to settle in Matabeleland, as they had been loyal to the British. This was the tribe to which John Radasi belonged.

Radasi made some initial contacts in the town (now city) of Bulawayo. He applied for and received ten acres of land in a nearby rural area known as Ingwenya, on which a church building, a school and a home were constructed. In addition to evangelistic work among the animistic people of the region, Radasi began primary school teaching and also some medical work. Ingwenya was in the Ntabazinduna Reserve (now "Area") but the work was later to expand deeper into the remote and heavily forested Shangani Reserve (now Nkai Area), where our future family home would one day be located.

*Miss Jean Nicolson*

In 1924 a Scottish minister, the Reverend John Tallach, was to join Radasi. When the new missionary arrived in Bulawayo, he was greeted with the news that Radasi, on his way to meet him, had been killed by an oncoming train at a railway siding near Ingwenya. Despite this tragic setback, the work continued, and two years later John Tallach was joined by Dr. Roderick MacDonald, who was both a medical doctor and an ordained minister. Ingwenya School was upgraded to a boarding school in 1933 on the arrival of Miss Jean Nicolson. It was as a temporary replacement for Miss Nicolson that my father entered the scene, while she was on home leave.

## PERSONAL BACKGROUND

James Fraser was born on the 17th of May 1913 in the picturesque Scottish Highland village of Strathpeffer,

21

just west of the county town of Dingwall, Ross-shire. He was a middle child with an older sister, Elizabeth (Betty), and a younger sister, Helen. His father owned a small but prosperous clothing business in the village and served as an elder in the Dingwall Free Presbyterian congregation. He was also a lay preacher "of marked ability whose services were valued in congregations throughout a wide area."[5] When my grandmother was a young woman, she had a strong desire to serve God in a capacity other than as a wife and mother. In due time, her prayers changed to the effect that her children would do so.

*My father's parents*

As a boy, my father's interests were more in the land and animals than in academics. Once when asked by his minister what he would like to be when he grew up, he answered, "A shepherd and an elder, please sir!" He used to spend his summers working on a farm owned by friends in the neighbouring county of Inverness-shire. Years later, I was to follow in that tradition and also, into my late teens, shared the desire to become a shepherd. Two memories from my own days on the farm stand out. Once I was told, "There's one difference between you and your father. He was a hard worker!" On another occasion, an elderly gentleman said, with tears in his eyes, "If you're half the man your father was, you'll be all right!"

*The family home in Strathpeffer, Scotland*

After a fairly undistinguished education at nearby primary and secondary schools, my father attended Glasgow University, where his academic abilities began to flourish. His arts degree included a first prize in Scottish history and the commendation "Would that other students had half your understanding!" This was followed by a teacher training course at Jordanhill

Training College (now part of the University of Strathclyde) in Glasgow and, for about two years after, by various teaching posts in Ross-shire schools.

It was during his Jordanhill days, while attending a communion season at his home church in Dingwall in 1935, that my father made a public profession of his faith. Three years later, he was approached about replacing Jean Nicolson for an eighteen-month period at the mission school in Southern Rhodesia and agreed to go.

*Dad with his sisters, Betty (left) and Helen*

*On the lawn at Timaru*

## BEGINNING MISSION WORK

On Friday the 15th of July 1938, he sailed from Southampton on the *Stirling Castle,* arriving at Cape Town, South Africa, on Thursday the 28th. The sea voyage was made more pleasant by the company of two other missionaries bound for the Congo. After disembarking at Cape Town and taking a two-day train journey to Bulawayo, my father was met by Mr. Tallach and Dr. MacDonald. Soon thereafter, life began at the mission school at Ingwenya. Preaching, as well as school teaching, soon became one of the duties at both Ingwenya and some of the outlying mission posts.

*The Reverend John Tallach*

The Rhodesian summer of 1938-39 was unusually wet. My father's biography contains a number of long, dramatic passages detailing the perils of driving in such conditions, then and in after-years. Here is one extract:

> The wet and slippery top skin of the roads creates one skid after another, all of which require instant correction if the car is not to plunge disastrously into the soft ground of the fields on either side...Round a bend you come, wrenching the wheel this way and that to keep the slithering rear wheels in approximately the centre of the track. To your horror a morass which stretches from side to side of the road comes rushing towards you. In the dry season you knew it as just a black patch on the road...Now its glis-

tening expanse appears to wait to seize the car in an oozy grip from which it cannot escape. Two very deep, water-filled ruts cleave the length of the slough...But you drive on, aiming your swaying chariot at the ruts...On either side a wave of black water rises and breaks into the ruts. The car lurches and squeals...A fear grips you that the flagging engine will never draw you through the quagmire and then with joy you realize that the revs are increasing again...One last, tremendous bone-shaking crash as the wheels enter and bounce out of a hole just where the ruts end and, with a great sense of relief and elation you are back on firmer ground with only the skids to worry about.[6]

*A "good" river crossing*

The end result was not always so happy. On some occasions vehicles had to be pulled by oxen out of mud-holes or even across a three-foot river that had days before been a dry grassy bed.[7]

When weather permitted, one of my father's few relaxations was hunting, a skill he had begun to develop on the hills of home. Years later, after our family had moved into the more remote Shangani Reserve, this was to stand us in good stead. The biography records,

> There were weeks on end when only his remarkable skill provided the fresh meat which was needed to keep not only his own family in health, but also the much larger family of boy boarders who, unless they had meat at least once a week, were very unhappy and indeed undernourished.[8]

Hunting proved to be not only a source of food, but also a means of protection. My sister Isobel is the custodian of a leopard skin given to our father as a gift from African villagers as thanks for his having killed the prowling animal. It had climbed a tree and was in the act of leaping at him when he shot it.

## TEACHING AT INGWENYA

Serving as head teacher was the main task at Ingwenya, taking over from Paul Hlazo, "one of several brothers who had from the beginning of the mission rendered it great service" and who had been acting head since Miss Nicolson's departure. After observing my father taking on his new responsibilities, Mr. Hlazo confided to John Tallach, "That chap can fairly teach." From one who was himself "no mean exponent of the art," the opinion "was a high compliment."[9]

*With Standard 6 at Ingwenya School, 1939*

During his time at Ingwenya, my father developed a lifelong friendship with James Stewart, a fellow Scot who was the government inspector of native schools. Once Mr. Stewart made a surprise visit to announce that pupils at Ingwenya had taken five out of eleven prizes for essays on "veld fires," in some cases competing against students two grades higher in other schools. Although the biography notes that he "did not so much as hint that his own efforts had contributed to this,"[10] when Jean Nicolson returned a little over a year later she observed in general that it was "very evident that Mr. Fraser had done his work with tremendous energy and success."[11]

A consequence of the publicity given to the essay results was a flood of applications to the school, but Mr. Tallach as mission superintendent had already been forced, due to space limitations, to reject quite a few. My father's comment on the situation was, "I believe that this place could become a really great educational and evangelistic centre, if only we had the funds to permit extension. Still, He who works in our midst knows our needs and what is best for the mission."[12]

## TEACHER TRAINING AT HOPE FOUNTAIN

The friendship with James Stewart was to influence the period following Miss Nicolson's return and the end of my father's temporary assignment. It had been his intention to return to Scotland, but in the meantime World War II had broken out, and there was little likelihood of securing an immediate passage to the homeland. Several other attractive options soon presented themselves, among them an offer to serve as master of methods at the teacher training school of the London Missionary Society at Hope Fountain, eleven miles south of Bulawayo and some forty miles from Ingwenya. Mr. Stewart was especially keen for him to accept the offer, and this was a factor in his deciding to do so. Work at Hope Fountain began in April 1940 and continued until after the war, when my father finally returned to Scotland.

It was during his time at Hope Fountain that he was given the nickname *Thandabantu* ("the man who loves the people"). "Very often these names describe some physical feature of the white persons to whom they are applied, but in his case the characteristic which the natives saw most strongly marked, was his love for them, a love many times proved and never negated by word or deed."[13]

He also quickly earned a reputation as indeed a master of teaching methods. In years to come, the teacher training centres in both government and mission circles were to be run on principles developed by him. As one African teacher is reported to have remarked, "Mr. Fraser can come into your classroom and by looking at your blackboard can tell whether or not you are a good teacher."14

*Teacher training students at Hope Fountain*

Just as at Ingwenya, my father added preaching and personal evangelism to his workload. During his third year at Hope Fountain, he took over regular open-air services at nearby Coronation Mine. In this he was replacing an American Baptist minister who had assisted in the teacher training work for a year but then left to engage in literature ministry.

Despite the many opportunities thus presented, along with early success in the work of teacher training—in 1941 Hope Fountain took first place in government examinations of five teacher training centres in Matabeleland—my father continued to think of home. In part this was due to anxiety about the war raging in Europe, but he was also concerned about his parents, who were approaching retirement. Besides the clothing business in Strathpeffer, they owned a large house, Timaru, in which much gospel hospitality had been shown, but it was time to downsize. The thought of taking over the business and the home was attractive, but as my father wrote to his mother, the other option was of "returning to labour among my black friends. The call...is a loud and urgent one, and it may be that it will one day sound so loudly in my ears that I shall have no other course than to answer it."

This is in fact what happened, but first my father's desire to assist in the war effort was such that he intended to resign from Hope Fountain after only a year. However, appeals originating from the mission superintendent resulted in a letter from the prime minister's office (dated 19th September 1941) requesting him to stay at his post, as it was "of the greatest national importance." Thus, it was not until September of 1945 that he returned to Scotland, after what had become a seven-year absence.

PART 2

WHILE AT HOME, MY FATHER STUDIED FOR AND WAS ordained to the church's ministry. In addition, he took a course in dentistry, which was to serve him well in years to come. Most importantly, from a family point of view, he married his childhood sweetheart, Christine (Chris) Finlayson, who had grown up in Dingwall, where her father (like her husband's) was an elder in the local Free Presbyterian church. Trained as a nurse, she had served during the war, treating wounded soldiers in a hospital in Belgium close to the battlefront. My parents were married in 1945, and in November of 1946 Elizabeth was born. In September 1947, the young family set sail for Africa and what was to be my parents' lifework.

From aboard ship, my father wrote of experiencing "a touch of homesickness":

*The newlyweds on the steps of Timaru*

The longing to sit with you at the old kitchen table, to hear Helen come in from the shop, to join you in the wee Kirk in Dingwall and to walk round the garden and to inspect the vegetable plots and the henyard was very strong indeed, but it was a great comfort to reflect on the happy times we have had together and to recall that He who has separated us will not be in debt to any of His children.

Twice before going to Hope Fountain and once while he was working there, my father had made exploratory trips into the large Shangani Reserve (now Nkai Area) to the northwest of Ingwenya. During his stay in Scotland, he had addressed the church's 1946 annual synod in these terms:

There is a cry from Africa going out to us here tonight, and the cry—a cry for help—is none the less real or urgent because it is not articulate. I have stood on one of the hills of the Shangani Reserve and have looked forth on, I believe, hundreds of square miles of forest and grassland, with the smoke of African villages rising in the evening air here and there among the trees, and I have felt almost overpowered by a realization of the enormity of our task as a missionary body, and yet when we think of the almighty power of God and the prayers of a sympathetic Church at home, we feel we can go on in the strength of God the Lord, and we feel too that our Church may yet be used more and more...

He closed by referring to an African travel companion, Paul Ncube:

Throughout the trip this man, who is of a very solid and unemotional type, had been very happy in his own quiet way. I said to him, "You looked very happy throughout the journey. Why were you so happy?" "Well," he said, "it is not so long ago since the Reserve was in total darkness, and

*Dad and Mum with Elizabeth*

even now there is only a little light, but the Word of God is in this Reserve and the Holy Spirit is at work here too, and there is no hope for the powers of darkness. Christ must prevail. The whole Reserve will yet be lit up with the Glory of

*Paul Ncube*

the Gospel of the Lord Jesus Christ." If we go forth in that spirit, we can be sure that the Lord will acknowledge our efforts.[15]

## ZENKA AND MBUMA

After a brief stay in Ingwenya, while a house was being built for them in Zenka, ninety miles to the north, my parents and sister moved to their new home. Another daughter, Isobel, was born in June 1949.

This is how Elizabeth remembers Zenka:

The house we lived in was built of bricks made from mud and hardened by drying in the sun. These were then plastered with mud. The inside was painted with a distemper whitewash. There was a veranda at the front, and behind it there was a dining-living room and a bedroom, with a pantry and a bathroom at the back. The kitchen was a separate hut behind the house, with a wood-burning stove, which often produced a lot of smoke, inside the kitchen as well as up the chimney.

At bath time, buckets of water were heated on top of the stove and emptied into a tin bath in the bathroom. Isobel and I were bathed together, once the tem- perature of the water

*Dad and Isobel*

was at a suitable level. After we were washed, the water was used for watering plants in the garden—presumably unharmed by the soapi- ness of the water. Water recycling was necessary when water had to be collected from a borehole some distance away. At the borehole, water had to be manually pumped up. One person could do this with difficulty, but help was always appreci- ated.

Another hut, a bit away from the house, was known as the dispensary. In it was kept a selec- tion of medicines, bandages, and needles and syringes. Our mother attended to a variety of ail- ments there and cleaned and dressed wounds. I have no clear memories of events in the dispensary during the Zenka days, although I used to go there to watch my mother as she went about her work. Years later, when we lived at Mbuma, we were at Zenka for a few days. My young brother Cameron was bitten by a very young but poisonous snake. In no time someone killed the snake, and my mother got out the anti-snakebite serum and gave Cameron an injection. He suffered no ill effects, apart from a little pain and fright.

*Helping hands at a borehole*

Elizabeth also notes that our mother would often tackle medical problems that would normally require a doctor.

In January 1954, the family moved farther into the forest to a more central location, Mbuma, where a teacher training centre was established to prepare teachers for the mission schools. It would be a mistake, however, to conclude that our father's work was focused exclusively on Zenka and then Mbuma. These were central locations from which over twenty "kraal schools" were operated in the surrounding areas on both sides of the Shangani River, necessitating many "treks" to supervise these schools. They also functioned as worship centres, and preaching as well as medical and dental services were provided on these visits.

*The house in Zenka*

A former student at Hope Fountain, Petros Mzamo, was to assist first as a teacher in Zenka and then at the teacher training school in Mbuma, while studying for the ministry under our father's tutelage. The teacher training work was also joined by Miss C.M. ("Katie Mary") Macaulay from Scotland. Following ordination in 1957, Mr. Mzamo shared in the preaching and pastoral ministry in Mbuma and vicinity.[16] Another African teacher, Aaron Ndebele, who succeeded Petros Mzamo as head of the Zenka school, would later become minister of the Ingwenya congregation. He passed away in 2004.

Mr. Mzamo retired after more than fifty years in the ministry. We were especially close to the Mzamo family, and their son Mbonisi was my first childhood friend.

*The Reverend Petros Mzamo had the distinction, in 1963, of being unanimously elected as the first African moderator of the Synod of the Free Presbyterian Church of Scotland and, for that matter, of the governing body of any Christian denomination in Scotland and likely the United Kingdom.*

## MISSIONARY PHILOSOPHY

Our parents and their colleagues believed that medicine and education were "handmaids" of the gospel, a view many missiologists today would dismiss as colonial-era thinking. In my father's biography there is a long quotation to the effect that Christian education is the hope of Africa. "...Church and school knit in an indissoluble unit was the ideal that John Knox established for Scotland, and that union has left a tremendous impress on the world. What Knox joined together let us not put asunder, and it will do the same for Africa..." wrote J.H. Hunter in 1961.[17]

John Knox's educational influence on Scotland and beyond is indisputable, but it is at least debatable whether it has had a similar effect on the structures of African society as a whole.[18] The reasons for this are complex. However, there can be no doubt that, within their own sphere of influence, much spiritual good was in fact done as a result of my parents' approach, both in medical and educations terms. For instance, several teachers trained by our father became primary school headmasters, and also "very many became members and elders in the Church, encouraging the spread of the gospel in their respective areas."[19] Some also entered the ministry.

## THE INFLUENCE OF CHRISTIAN EDUCATION

The example given here is from the earlier period of our father's work in Ingwenya. In a report to the 1939 synod in Scotland, he first gave some examples of the questions asked and answers provided in Scripture examinations and then continued:

More gratifying even than good answers, is the influence for good which these Christian girls exert upon a wider circle of their acquaintances. Their usefulness as witnesses for Christ among their companions in school and at their homes is real and far-reaching. An indication of what they do in their homes is given in a letter which Mr. Tallach received during the December holidays from the father of a girl who at one time had been most troublesome, but since September has given unmistakable evidence of a definite change in her life. Her father wrote to Mr. Tallach informing him that he was sending his daughter back to school at Ingwenya because her previous sojourn at the Mission had effected a very pleasing change in her conduct. She had ceased to be disobedient to her mother, her manner had become bright and pleasant, and she had insisted that family worship be held in the home twice every day. Through her influence also, her brothers and sisters had begun to read their Bibles and to treat their parents with kindness and respect. The same happy results are evident in the school when a number of girls come under the power of the Holy Spirit and when the change of heart and outlook which follows is brought to bear upon the details of school life. Since March last year about fifty girls have been received for baptism...[20]

Later, towards the end of my father's career, the biography aptly indicates his attitude:

Much of James' time was undoubtedly taken up with tasks which could be called secular, but he was always ready to point out that everything he did had a close and real connection with his primary design to extend the Redeemer's kingdom in Shangani...It could...be said of the educational side that it was a means to an end, an indispensable means. No schools—no congregations! No schools—no Bible reading and instruction! No training centres—no properly qualified teachers, and no teachers versed in true doctrine or trained to teach it!...James accepted all the various parts of his work as necessary; what he regretted was that he was compelled for lack of helpers to devote to the auxiliary tasks the time and energy which he would have preferred to spend in the work peculiar to the Christian ministry.

He liked teaching; but he loved to preach and teach the Gospel of the Kingdom. He liked treating the ailments and hurts of men's bodies, but he liked nothing better than the more exacting work of treating their souls' diseases.[21]

## MEDICINE AND MAZWABO

Once when our father expressed concern that people were attracted to worship services less by the preaching than by the medicines distributed afterwards, George Ndebele, an African lay preacher, remarked, "Don't let us worry too much about that. The medicines preach too."[22]

An example of the use of medicine as a "handmaid" of the gospel is illustrated in the story of Mazwabo. One day a small, wizened old African woman arrived at the clinic in Zenka. She was dressed in rags and was "extremely dirty." She had burned her foot at a cooking fire, and through lack of attention it was now septic and foul smelling, "a large, angry sore surrounded by thick dirt." (My sister Elizabeth developed a fascination with Mzwabo and, unless prevented, would snuggle up against her "verminous" body.)

Father (who, along with doing dentistry work, sometimes assisted Mother) got down on his knees and began cleaning Mazwabo's foot, all the time speaking to her in Ndebele "of the wounds and sicknesses of her soul which were so much worse than even her foot." She "seemed to have no understanding at all of the fact that she had a soul needing to be cleansed. All her concern was for her sore foot and her empty stomach."[23]

After some weeks of "apparently impenetrable deafness" to our father's exhortations, Mazwabo came to church. Noticing that the other women wore dresses, she expressed a desire for one. Our mother made her a dress and a headband out of a curtain. Father asked, "Would you like to see yourself in your dress, Mazwabo?" As one author describes the scene:

> She would, and they went into his house. "There, Mazwabo, look in that long mirror and you will see how nice you look!" She approached the said object somewhat cautiously and then sprang back in terror. "What is that? It's moving!" and she cowered in the farthest corner. Assuring her it was no spirit she had glimpsed, Mr. Fraser

gradually coaxed her to venture near once again. After several abortive attempts she got there. The dress truly was beautiful, she said, but oh, how ugly she was! Perhaps she was, but when she became a Christian she had a bright happy expression that lent beauty to her features.[24]

How Mazwabo became a Christian is described by my father in his 1949 report to the church's synod in Scotland:

> After nine months of diligently seeking, the way of salvation was revealed to her in a brilliant flash of mercy. Ever since... Mazwabo has been an entirely different person. All her interests now are bound up in the Gospel... Her very expression is more pleasing and her mind which was formerly a blank to all except food and drink, is now occupied with a variety of interests, all centring in the things of God.

*Group photo with Mazwabo in the foreground and Dad and Aunt Margaret directly behind her*

Not long ago, Petros Mzamo and I visited the miserable kraal at which Mazwabo lives and found all but herself in a drunken stupor. "Do you ever speak to these people about their souls,

45

Mazwabo?" we asked. "Do I ever speak to them
about their souls!" she exclaimed. "I am never
done speaking to them but they won't listen to
me. When I start telling them about Jesus, they
say, 'If you want to talk on that subject, go and do
so with your father the missionary.' When they
answer me like that I just go into my hut and
pray."

In a later report, Mazwabo is mentioned again:

She was frequently taunted, and even thrashed,
for refusing to take part in the custom of praying
to the spirits of her ancestors...The beer-drinks
which accompany these devotions have, since her
conversion, been an abomination to her and
whenever they began, Mazwabo invariably
sought asylum in the home of some Christian
family...She now lives with a distant relative
whose home is fully three miles from the mission,
but in spite of distance and advancing years,
Mazwabo never misses a service unless she is ill.
Her consistent witness for the Saviour is a source
of encouragement to the Church at Zenka.[25]

When our father's biography was published in 1967,
someone showed Mazwabo a copy. She turned the pages
till she came to a photograph of him. With a sad face,
she said "Nang ubaba" ("Here is Father"). Then her face
lit up, and, with a hand pointing heavenwards, she said,
"He is up there in heaven. When I die my body will be
buried in the earth, but my soul will go to be with the
Lord and with ubaba."[26]

*A typical African kraal, consisting of a number of huts, together with an enclosure for cattle*

PART 3

I WAS BORN IN AUGUST OF 1954, A YEAR THAT BEGAN WITH my parents and sisters moving from Zenka to Mbuma in the Shangani Reserve, where our father started a teacher training centre and our mother continued her medical work. The biography notes that I "bore a strong resemblance" to my father and "became attached to him with an unusual strength of affection that is not difficult to understand."[27]

In this section, my intention is to provide more of a personal and family perspective than is available in the biography or various other published sources.[28] This will necessitate missing out a number of details available elsewhere, including the important work of several African and European colleagues, such as my father's biographer, Alexander McPherson, who was in charge of construction on the mission from 1947-54 and later became a minister in Scotland. I mean no disrespect to

*Mum and the children*

these individuals, for many of whom I retain the highest regard, not least for the memory of "Auntie Jean" Nicolson, whose own remarkable life has recently been recorded.[29] Then there was James Tallach, son of the mission's first European superintendent, who replaced Mr. McPherson. I was always impressed at how James could drive all kinds of vehicles with his eyes shut. Only years later did I discover that while his eye next to me appeared to be firmly shut, the other was wide open! My attachment to James Tallach can be gauged from a letter my father wrote to family at home: "James is still with us but expects to return to Ingwenya tomorrow. Cameron says he is going with him and has packed a box with bars of soap, cake tins and toy cars in readiness!"

## MEMORIES OF MBUMA

I asked both of my sisters to provide me with their African memories. Elizabeth's recollections of Zenka have already been given. Here is what she has written about Mbuma:

> The house in Mbuma, which we moved to after we came back from a year's home leave, was much more substantial than the house at Zenka. It was bigger, had more rooms, was made of cement bricks, and had cement floors that were covered with linoleum, and we had a carpet in the living room. We also had running water. Such luxury was quite exciting! However, our journey getting there on moving day was not exactly exciting! We got stuck in mud on the road (a frequent occurrence during the rainy season), and the lorry we were in was so loaded with furniture, etc., that we had to spend the night in the cab of the lorry, until help came at daylight! Two adults and two children in the cab of a lorry didn't make for a comfortable night's sleep—at least for the adults!
>
> My father was always busy, but he made the effort to spend time with his children and to instruct us in an interesting way. He only had to ask us once to do, or not to do, something. He was firm, but kind and loving with it. He had a strong sense of humour, often seeing the funny side of an incident when others would not be aware of any humour in it.
>
> He taught during the week and preached at least twice every Sunday, occasionally taking an extra

service at what were called outstations, some distance away. The services in the outstations were taken in a one-roomed school, usually with a mud floor, and very uncomfortable backless benches to sit on. I remember going with him on one occasion and being relieved when the service was over because I was so uncomfortable. Although he spoke in Ndebele, I could usually follow the gist of what was said, because he made his message simple for people who were not used to hearing sermons.

*The house in Mbuma*

Our dad encouraged an interest in nature study, and I was able to identify and name the local trees and some of the birds. He also encouraged an interest in animals, and we had the responsibility of feeding young turkey chicks with mashed up hard-boiled hens' eggs. We enjoyed looking after newborn lambs if their mothers did not have enough milk. Because we were over a hundred miles away from shops where we could get fresh food, we had to be self-sufficient to some extent, so the sheep, hens and turkeys we had usually ended up feeding us and the African pupils in the boarding school. The pigs were taken away and sold; they were never butchered at Mbuma. (We may only have had one lot of pigs. I think they were difficult to keep.) There were cows and calves too, mainly to provide us all with milk and, occasionally, with meat. Meat was also provided when Dad went off to the forest, accompanied by a dog, to shoot a small buck or a much bigger kudu.[30]

*The "big tree" near Mbuma—this baobab measures 80 ft. in circumference.*

Our mother taught Isobel and me, guiding us as we worked through the lessons sent from the correspondence school in Salisbury (now Harare). She also had a busy life, looking after us and working in the dispensary, where she treated a variety of ailments and occasionally delivered a baby whose mother was having difficulties. One thing she didn't do was extract teeth! This was done by our father.

It is to our mother's credit that Isobel and I were both able to join "A" classes when we came to Scotland following our father's death.[31] However, we both enjoyed reading, and we made use of the arrival of someone at the dispensary needing her help to disappear off to our bedroom with a book or go to the nearby (dried up most of the year) stream to play in the sand or jump onto it from a high part of the bank. This must have been quite frustrating for her, and I am sure she must have

*The three children outside the house in Mbuma*

wished we had the perseverance to carry on with our work on our own.

Isobel adds these memories of our father in Mbuma:

Running to meet him as he came back from the school: I carried his books for him—usually just a small bundle he held in his hand—and felt pleased that I was helping him...

Washing his feet after he had been out hunting or on trek: I had a little nurse's uniform and put that on before I washed his feet in a basin. Again, I felt so proud that I was of use to him. Whether I was or not, that's the impression I was left with!...

The excitement of welcoming him home after he had been away one time in Salisbury: He brought me back a Brer Rabbit book, which I loved...

Being encouraged to plant flower seeds in the garden: Elizabeth and I were given a packet of seeds. We decided one of us would have the top half, the other the bottom half, of the packet. He was listening but left us to find out our mistake for ourselves!...

Him playing with us after bath and supper: I think it was a regular occurrence, though it might have been quite brief. I remember him on hands and knees and us climbing on his back...

We often went with him, too, when he went to visit a nearby kraal. There was nothing special for us to do; we just played around or waited while he talked to people, but presumably he was making an effort to include us in his day, and we wanted to go...

He used to read to us on Sunday afternoons. I remember *Pilgrim's Progress* and stories from the Reformation...He also used to take us to feed the pigs (giving the boys who normally did it a day off), and we would sit on rocks in the dry bed of the stream and learn our psalm and catechism...I remember him once asking a question, something like "Who is our Redeemer?" I knew the answer fine, but for some reason I responded with a flippant "I don't know." He was really grieved by that and spoke earnestly about Jesus and what he had done for us...We used to sing hymns on a Sunday evening, sometimes at least.

## PREMATURE DEATHS

Two years after my birth, a younger brother was stillborn. Our mother had been in poor health for some time, exacerbated by malaria attacks. Elizabeth remembers:

She had contracted hepatitis from a patient she looked after some time before she was married. According to an aunt, she went back to work too soon, and her liver did not get the chance to heal properly. Each pregnancy she had, and the difficult lifestyle on the mission, put increasing strain on her damaged liver. Latterly, she was often in pain and had to avoid certain foods. The damage eventually led to liver failure, which resulted in her death at the age of forty-four.

*Last time together in Scotland*

Our father, three years her senior, died two years before her, worn out from a workload that he once described as "carrying a burden greater than any mortal man can bear."[32] For some time he had suffered from severe sinus headaches as well as bouts of malaria. Then sometime in 1958, we went on a family holiday to Victoria Falls, along with our Aunt Margaret, who had come over two years previously to help Mother and then began nursing in the city of Bulawayo, 120 miles to the south. She remembers (as do I) that while at the falls, our father was bitten by a monkey while retrieving a child's ball from a tree:

> Several months later [he] became ill with flu-like symptoms. Chris [our mother] was alarmed. She

was the only white person at Mbuma, and there was no one who could drive the truck. In the Lord's gracious providence, James Tallach arrived after a difficult trip [and then] went back to Bulawayo to get medical advice and help.

*A section of Victoria Falls*

Our father was taken by ambulance to the hospital in Bulawayo, where our aunt remembers being on duty and admitting him as a patient. "We were relieved and grateful that he had got there safely and thought all would be well now." However, after only a few months, he passed away on the 28th of March 1959, from what remained a mysterious illness.[33] Jean Nicolson expressed the thoughts of many: "His gain—our loss; but also, I feel, a warning to us not again to allow a young, enthusiastic missionary to be so overworked."[34] Some 2,000 people, mostly Africans, attended the funeral, which was held in Ingwenya.

*The date on the gravestone is incorrect.*
*It should be 28th March 1959.*

Our parents had been overdue for home leave, and arrangements had already been made. With our aunt, the remaining family continued on to Scotland. Aunt Margaret recalls:

> During the voyage home we were looking at a beautiful sunset. I said, "James would have enjoyed such a spectacular view."
> "Don't say that!" Chris retorted. "What he is seeing now far surpasses anything he ever saw here on earth." I felt rebuked and fully agreed.

Both of our maternal grandparents and our paternal grandfather had gone to be with the Lord. We settled in our mother's hometown of Dingwall, sharing a house with our father's mother and our Aunt Helen. In 1961, our mother passed away. Among her papers was found a note beginning, with typical understatement, "I don't feel well." It continued (slightly edited for punctuation, but not content):

> If I am suddenly taken away, don't let anyone mourn. Above all, do not wear black. To my children I say, "Strive to enter in at the Strait Gate." None who seek the Lord are ever denied Him. You are my only concern. Not your eternal welfare; that I have committed to the Lord—so too your welfare here—so why am I concerned? I am not concerned; I just feel sorry that I am leaving you because I know you will miss me, for a time at any rate. Think of me as forever with the Lord and to a lesser degree with Daddy. You too will come to this glorious place. Seek in the meantime to do all things for God's glory and do well anything that you have to do.[35]

My mother's confidence in our eternal welfare has been a source of comfort through the years.

# EPILOGUE

IN THE TWO YEARS FOLLOWING OUR FATHER'S DEATH, EIGHT new workers left Scotland for the mission to which he had devoted his life, "in which fact the lesson is again read to us by the God of providence and grace that He depends on no one particular agent to perform His work."[36] It is beyond the purpose of this short book to bring the story any further up to date. I would, however, like to mention Jan van Woerden, who became our uncle when he married Aunt Margaret (after she returned to the mission). He had actually arrived before our father's death and was at Zenka to begin with but moved to Mbuma, as requested by our father before his death.

In addition to administrative responsibilities, Jan, as a trained nurse, developed our mother's medical work to the point that by 1961 there was an outpatient department and two hospital wards, now considerably expanded. He was assisted by our aunt, to whom he was

then engaged, and in 1961 Catherine Tallach (sister to
James) joined the work. Catherine's younger sister,
Margaret, arrived in 1967 as part of a growing staff.
Then another James Tallach, third son of our father's
sister Betty, became the first doctor in Mbuma in 1969.

*James Tallach (right) was the first doctor at
Mbuma Mission Hospital.*

Uncle Jan was also the means of introducing the mission to Dutch churches, resulting in the formation of
Mbuma Zending (Mission), with the provision of considerable financial assistance and now a mainly Dutch staff
in Mbuma. The financial assistance was especially prov-
idential during the years of Ian Smith's illegal regime
when the British placed sanctions on Rhodesia, limiting
the amount of funds that could be sent from there.

The van Woerdens moved on for a time to engage in
non-denominational literature ministry and later
(1976) the founding, in Bulawayo, of Thembiso, the first
children's home of its kind in Matabeleland, now oper-

ated by the Free Presbyterian Church and needed more than ever in this age of AIDS orphans.[37]

*The van Woerden family with staff and children at Thembiso*

When my father died, I was four and a half, an age at which most young boys idolize their fathers. My mother wrote in a letter home that "Cameron is too young to remember what a daddy he had," but my memories, though few and scattered, are vivid and lasting.

As an adult I have on occasion wondered if my recollections of family life with Father were perceived through the rose-coloured spectacles of a child, but my sisters have assured me that this is not so. His obvious attempts to include us in his work, as well as to spend family time with us, are, I believe, one reason why we have not gone through the periods of bitterness and rebellion all too often experienced by the children of missionaries and others devoted to a "higher calling."

I am aware that there were struggles, discouragements and disappointments from which we were shielded. "During the closing years of his life," the biography recounts, he "was often assailed with the temptation to give up his work." Uncle Jan told the biographer that "at this time James felt so weak and burdened that he was on the point of resigning."[38] The picture I have presented is thus incomplete, but it is accurate. It is the picture I would like to leave with my own sons and others interested in my father's life and legacy.

Let me end with two quotations. The first is from an African school headmaster at the time of my father's death:

> This brilliant man, how modest! Please tell Scotland that in James she gave us her best...I happen to know how deeply and widely mourned he is by the African people in this part of the country. Please tell Scotland that James Fraser's elevation to a higher service is a terrible challenge to the African people here and to Scotland herself. Scotland's sons and daughters must come out quickly to carry on Mr. Fraser's work. This work must not lag behind, must not fail, because it cannot fail.[39]

Then there are the closing words of the biography, published in 1967 but still relevant:

> All who have a heart interest in foreign missions ought now to be pleading with the Lord of the harvest that He would raise up and send out labourers of the calibre of the Rev. James Fraser. That would be to pray for something great and rare, but 'Is anything too hard for the Lord?'[40]

# ENDNOTES

[1] Alexander McPherson, *James Fraser: A Record of Missionary Endeavour in Rhodesia in the Twentieth Century* (London: Banner of Truth, 1967).

[2] For a revealing account of life under Mugabe by a former supporter, see Judith Garfield Todd, *Through the Darkness: A Life in Zimbabwe* (Zebra Press, Cape Town, 2007).

[3] Jean Nicolson, *John Boyana Radasi: Missionary to Zimbabwe* (Glasgow: Free Presbyterian Publications, 1996), pp. 10-11.

[4] The early history of Matabeleland is told by Peter Becker in *Path of Blood: The Rise and Conquests of Mzilikazi founder of the Matabele tribe of Southern Africa* (London: Longmans, 1962).

[5] McPherson, pp. 3-4.

[6] Ibid., p. 30.

7 See "Mbuma School Report" by Miss K.M. Macaulay in *Proceedings of Synod of the Free Presbyterian Church of Scotland* (1957), p. 75.

8 McPherson, p. 31.

9 Ibid., p. 18.

10 Ibid., p. 26.

11 *History of the Free Presbyterian Church of Scotland (1893-1970)* (Inverness: Pub. Committee), p. 217.

12 McPherson, pp. 26-27.

13 Ibid., p. 117.

14 Quoted in an obituary in the *Free Presbyterian Magazine,* vol. LXV (1960-61), p. 20.

15 McPherson, pp. 127-8.

16 The late F.F. Bruce, in reviewing histories of the Free Church and Free Presbyterian Church, noted that "the Free Presbyterian Church showed itself well in advance of the current climate of opinion when, in 1963, it unanimously elected the Rev. Petros Mzamo... to be Moderator of Synod—the first occasion on which an African presided over the supreme court of any Church in Scotland, or possibly in the whole United Kingdom" (*Evangelical Quarterly,* vol. 47, [1975], p. 245).

17 Quoted in McPherson, p. 58. In a 1949 "School Report—Ingwenya," Jean Nicolson stated that the "three chief aims of our educational work are, first, the conversion of the children; secondly, the training of those young people of more than average ability and character, as leaders and moulders of public opinion;

and thirdly, the raising of the masses to a decent standard of living."

18 One contemporary Zimbabwean and former mission school teacher (unrelated to the Free Presbyterian mission) with whom I have corresponded about this suggests, "As far as the Christian school, in my opinion, it has only a temporal/interim role to play in any reformation. I see the generational impact coming from faithful families where the father and mother are instructed and in turn instruct their children. This is slow in the beginning, but the compounding multiplication will have generational impact and the focus and emphasis is placed where I believe Scripture places it" (personal correspondence from Derek Carlsen).

19 Personal correspondence from C.M. Macaulay.

20 McPherson, pp. 43-4.

21 Ibid., p. 209.

22 "Shangani Mission Report" (1952), p. 37.

23 McPherson, p. 132. The reference to Mazwabo's "verminous" body is from one of my father's letters.

24 Dolina MacCuish, *A Heart for Africa: The story of Jean Nicolson-Missionary in Zimbabwe* (Glasgow: Free Presbyterian Publications, 2008), p. 191.

25 "Shangani Mission Report" (1950), pp. 56-7. Later, Mazwabo lived at Mbuma, where she died in 1968.

26 From an article by "J.N." (Jean Nicolson) in the *Free Presbyterian Magazine,* April 1998.

27 McPherson, pp. 211-2.

28 Besides the biography, see *History of the Free*

*Presbyterian Church of Scotland 1893-1970* (Inverness: Publications Committee, n.d.) (both out of print) and Dolina McCuish, *A Heart for Africa: The story of Jean Nicolson-Missionary to Zimbabwe* (Glasgow: Free Presbyterian Publications, 2008).

[29] See previous note.

[30] My father wrote, "The children, like myself, are very fond of birds and animals, especially Elizabeth and Cameron. I bought a duck from an old woman two weeks ago just to help her. It was intended for the pot right away, but thanks to the children's pleading it is still in the land of the living. Cameron always says, 'Daddy, if you buy a sheep you mustn't kill it. If you need meat you can go out and kill a buck in the forest.'"

[31] Isobel was "dux" (valedictorian) of the primary division at Dingwall Academy. She completed secondary school a year early.

[32] McPherson, p. 215.

[33] My cousin James Tallach recently wrote concerning my father's mysterious illness: "I did speak to the physician who attended your dad in his last illness. He died of hospital staphylococcal bacterial endocarditis, which damaged his heart valves and led to heart failure. They sent for Vancomycin, which was the only drug the bacterium was sensitive to, but it was too late by the time it arrived. However this was only one of the major events in his terminal illness, and Dr. She, the consultant, did not give any further opinion on how a strong man suffered such a series of major medical events and succumbed despite their best attentions. Cameron is probably right to speak of 'a mystery illness'

so long as it is clear that 'mystery' means only that it was not diagnosed at the time." In a subsequent response to a query from me, James added, "Though some question transmission by a monkey bite and 1959 is early for a case of AIDS, it is a distinct possibility that your dad's basic illness was AIDS."

34 MacCuish, p. 163.

35 There was also a note to our grandmother, quoting Jesus, "What you have done unto one of the least of these you have done unto me." We went to live with our mother's older sister, Ella, and her husband, the Reverend D.A. Macfarlane, a noted Free Presbyterian minister whose life and ministry is recorded by John Tallach in *I Shall Arise: the Life and Ministry of D.A. Macfarlane* (Aberdeen: Faro Publishing, 1984), with a personal appreciation from me.

36 McPherson, p. 221.

37 The vision for Thembiso (humanly speaking) initially came from my aunt.

38 McPherson, p. 217. This quote is from a later period, but there was an earlier one in the late 1940s and early '50s when a rising tide of nationalism, led it seems by Edwin Radasi, son of the mission's founder, gave rise to accusations against the white missionaries, in particular my father and Jean Nicolson. Radasi left the mission, taking several people with him, and formed a rival congregation. I met him years later in 1974, when he struck me as a gracious and dignified (then) older man, and relations with Miss Nicolson in particular seemed to be cordial, but he and others had been a source of considerable grief in earlier days.

[39] Quoted in a tribute in the *North Star* (30th May 1959) and reprinted in the *Free Presbyterian Magazine,* vol. LXIV (1959-60), pp. 119-20.

[40] McPherson, p. 221.